D0364118

Ordinary Beauty

Ordinary Beauty

Meaningful Moments in Everyday Life

MARY McEVOY

HACHETTE
BOOKS
IRELAND

Mary McEvoy is one of Ireland's best-loved and most acclaimed television and theatre actresses. She was born in Westmeath where she still lives, dividing her time between media, working her farm and acting.

Her memoir *How the Light Gets In: My Journey with Depression* was nominated for the BGE John Murray Listeners' Choice Award 2011.

First published in 2014 by Hachette Books Ireland

ISBN 978 1444 785 876

Book Design and Typesetting by Anú Design
Printed and bound by Clays Ltd, St Ives plc

Hachette Books Ireland policy is to use papers that are natural, renewable
and recyclable products and made from wood grown in sustainable forests.
The logging and manufacturing processes are expected to conform to the
environmental regulations of the country of origin.

Hachette Books Ireland
8 Castlecourt Centre
Castleknock
Dublin 15, Ireland

A division of Hachette UK Ltd.
338 Euston Road
London NW1 3BH

www.hachette.ie

To Garvan

Contents

Introduction

I chose *Ordinary Beauty* as the title for this book because
it is not about transcendence but about living in the
mundane world.

'Buddhism is daily life.' This is an adage I have
lived by for the last twenty-six years. Twenty-six years
of twice-daily prayers and constant self-examination.
I always thought I knew what it meant: 'Buddhism is
daily life.' It means you live your life as best you can.
It means that it is not just about prayers, morning and
evening, it is about constant vigilance. It means watching
your behaviour and striving always to correct it. And so
I have lived in this way. I was my own headmistress —
watching, berating, correcting. If I could just correct
a behaviour, I would be a 'good Buddhist'. I would
learn whatever lesson I needed to learn, and I would
be happy.

Side by side with this Calvinist approach to
Buddhism, my worldly desires have continued to run
wildly. I have always had grand dreams and ambitions,
which have only ever been partially realised. I have
always wanted to be better, thinner, richer, prettier.

I have longed for glamour and adventure, always assuming that where I was and what I was just wasn't enough. I believe that this inability to accept myself and my life, both spiritual and worldly, was one of the primary causes of the depression that has dogged me for so many years.

My depression slowly took hold in my thirties and forties, but it was in my fifties that it really became embedded. I began to feel I was running out of time. Time to live and time to be happy, or at least content. I was no longer young, I had lived more of my life than was left to live. I really had to find peace before it was too late. So I decided to really turn and face the 'enemy'. Running away and thinking from the outside in hadn't yielded the prize of enlightened ease, so maybe inside out was the way to deal with it.

So I started to look into my deeply held beliefs about everything. My family, my friends, my relationship, Buddhism, work, time, space, eternity but mainly myself. Who am I when all things are stripped away? All the provisional identities I have — woman, actress, Irish, success, failure, happy, sad, spiritual seeker, sensation junkie, lover, hater, kind, peevish, good, bad … What am I when I sit with nothing? Who am I when I stop yearning? When I stop trying to make things happen?

The beguiling and frustrating answer is: Damned if I know. That may seem like a negative statement but, for me, it was the beginning of freedom. Far from being a frightening discovery, this non-realisation was a wonderful relief. I was a speck whirling through time and space, confounded by the immensity of it, beaten down by experience and entranced by the mystery of it all. That's all.

So I began to sit with this 'not knowingness'. After a while, the sense of yearning and grasping, that wanting to have something I couldn't have or be something I couldn't be, started to settle. After a while, where I was and what I was, was enough. I haven't become enlightened, I am still a lost soul, and I tend to slip back into that grasping that the Tibetans call the hungry ghost quite often but, somehow, I get myself back to the sanity of being content to live the mystery of life, not solve it.

As always happens when a life lesson is learned, I did not plan it. I found myself more in the right place at the right time.

In November 2013, I joined a group of women in a cottage at the foot of Lough Crew in County Meath. We had gathered to celebrate the feast of Samhain, the Celtic new year. There were no fireworks or trick or treating or ducking for apples because, contrary to the modern belief about Hallowe'en and the time around it, Samhain is a quiet time. A time for going inward, a time for reflection. We sat and talked quietly about life and the meaning of it. We laughed gently and ate cake. At the end of the gathering, a woman used a Tibetan singing bowl to bring us into meditation. Its sound echoed in the warm room and we sat in silence for a long time. It was a wild evening, and the wind and rain howled and battered at the windows. When a realisation comes, it is hard to describe it, but I will try. In that silence with those women on that furious evening, it felt right, complete. I can't give a meaning to it because it just was. I don't even know what 'it' is. It is. That's all. That is what ordinary beauty is trying to point at. The 'suchness' of everything.

Pain, loss, love, youth, beauty, age, trees, birds, even ugliness, all take their place in the right order. It is perfect just as 'it' is. It is when we try to change, and manipulate 'it' to suit our own ego-bound agenda, that pain arises. So I am in the process of letting go all the provisional identities I wrote of earlier. Of trying to regain my lost and very deeply buried humility. It is not an easy task.

By letting go, I do not mean giving up. I still have my dreams and I want to be all that I can be. It would be a sin not to self-actualise, so great is the gift of life. I just want to move with life rather than pull against it. This I believe enables me to let go and not give up at the same time.

In letting go, I find I have become more alert to the beauty of life. Of everything. I see more when I manage to get out of my own way. The innocence of people when doing no harm and the beauty of the natural world. I enjoy the fun of watching my dog as he lives his doggy life, of giving voice to a straight-laced little hen who isn't too gone on sex. I embrace the sheer joy of deciding to be silly. I watch little dramas as they happen, on the streets and roads and fields. Instead of hating my kitchen, I can see the extraordinary in a boiling potato ... not always, but it has happened.

This morning, as I battle with the need to write and the desire to eat cake, that phrase – 'Buddhism is daily life' – is running around my mind. But today, it is accompanied by another: 'No affairs of life or work are separate from the ultimate reality.' These sayings are pulling me up again.

Recently, I heard myself say to a friend, 'I want my whole life to be a prayer.' I knew I didn't mean a sort of Holy Mary, no-fun kind of life. A bit like my old life that I had let go, when I was my own prison guard. No, I feel I am being drawn to a life of joyful participation. I am beginning to think that that's what these two Buddhist sayings mean. 'Buddhism is daily life', could that mean that what is happening all the time is 'it', is God, is Buddhism? 'No affairs of life or work are separate from the ultimate reality', does that mean that everything from buttering your toast to giving birth is a sacred act, an act of prayer?

The only problem then is negative acts – killing, bullying, hurting – are they prayers? Of course they are. They are prayers of negativity. They are prayers of separation. Separation from 'it'.

'Strive to cultivate the treasures of the heart' is another Buddhist adage. Now, I think I've got it: In the heart, there is no separation. When we lead with the heart, we see 'us' instead of 'them'. We see our selves as part of everything, rather than separate from it. In slowing down and letting go, I stopped obeying my ego. That part of me that wants to be somebody, the part of me that wants to say 'look at me' all the time. In slowing down and letting go, I led with my heart. I took my place in the universe rather than vainly trying to carve it out. It's restful here. I like it. My heart feels at home.

Now I have come to realise that nothing makes me happier than expressing love. Not because I'm a saint, I would hate that, but because my heart is being listened to at last, and that is what my heart wants. To express love is not just the words or the action. For me, it is seeing. Seeing the divinity in ordinary things – to see a water hen and delight in its presence or to see a bit of life unfolding on a street and be entranced by it.

The world's churches, mosques and temples are indeed beautiful sacred places, but worship can also take place in a hen house as the little feathery beings go about their chickeny lives. The feeling of a November evening as I gather sticks can be as sacred as a high mass. To imagine my dog's life is to love him for what he is. Because underneath all the differences lies the heart that just wants to love. This sounds so holy, I'm making myself sick. I'm not holy and I have so many flaws they are beyond counting. I still swear and have been known to gossip, I sometimes drink too much and eat too much and spend too much. I can scare myself with how mean-minded I can be.

I won't give up, however, and, as my days on earth pass, I get more adept at seeing my flaws as a witness does. When some meanness arises in me, I look at it as though I'm in a helicopter flying high above it and say, 'Now isn't that interesting? I didn't know I could be so peevish.' And the meanness passes through me — noticed, but not acted upon. The only thing that is certain for me is that I want to love and learn, and try to leave this planet with more kindness and wisdom than I came in with. And I want to pray. Pray like 'Hallelujah' by Leonard Cohen, for I would rather a broken hallelujah than a self-righteous one.

For all my flaws and weaknesses, gripes and anger, I'm part of this great, immense, unfathomable cosmic pattern, as we all are. That has sweetness in it. That has hope in it. To keep going, no matter what, to keep trying to love and laugh and pray, in other words to keep living until I die.

After that, who knows?

Here and now is enough, don't you think?

Mary McEvoy
July 2014

Loneliness

Introduction

I feel lonely quite a lot. In this section, I speak from my heart about the forms of loneliness that I experience. In these episodes, however, there is always consolation. Little pigeons, a cup of tea, a water hen. There are also lessons. Don't run. Stay and look. There is a gateway in that black wall. Wait. Things resolve themselves.

Perception is everything. I use the analogy of a temple, though I'm not sure it is an analogy. Most loneliness, I believe, is a longing for self. Not the self-involved self but the self that wants to love. This is the temple. I don't know if it is there, but I believe it is.

I am alone this morning. Love has left me.
It may not be forever, but I do not know. I don't
know what to do. My mind is frantic. Nothing makes
sense. I've been here before. The pain, the isolation
and the fear-driven ramblings of my racing mind.
One thing is different, however. I now know that
the way to freedom is through pain, not away from
it. Somewhere in my being, I sense the existence of a
temple. Dusty and unkempt, but it is there. I think.
I must find it, tend it. And love it into life.

Love has so many identities. The love of parents, spouses, siblings. The heady love of youth, the mellow love of age. The love of passion, all fiery and insatiable, the subtle love of maturity. The love one person has for another for no particular reason.

When fear melts, all that is left is love. In the depths of ourselves all beings long to love, I truly believe that. The worst of us, the most perverse and evil, the lost and angry, the sad and hopeless all scratch at life's breast in the hope of discovering love. One day, a boy racer nearly ran me off the road. I saw his face as I struggled to control my car, he looked so angry and desolate that whatever feelings of fear or anger I had towards him melted into, yes, I will say it, love.

When life is pulling you under, and you need to love something, I suggest you find a cat — if you are sensible enough to like cats. Place the cat before you and stroke it from the roundness of its head across its satiny back, right to the end of its sinuous tail. Repeat this process until calm. Sometimes, the cat will roll over offering its fluffy soft belly — the cat who lives with me boasts an underside of pale apricot — you have now been offered something rare, the trust of this slinky, secretive creature. Don't abuse it. Because the sacred lives in that soft fur.

I arrived in the radio station and took my usual seat.
I waited to do my job, tired and isolated. Lonely.
I was lost inside my pain.

'Mary, would you like a cup of tea?'

The young man hovered over me gentle and smiling.
His name wasn't Michael or Gabriel but his action
was angelic.

'Yes, I would.'

He could have offered me diamonds and they would
not have been more welcome. The simplest kindness
can have huge repercussions. And it was a lovely
cup of tea.

All I want is to be able to sit and read a book and be content. So far, this dream has eluded me. I long to breathe out. That long breath that says now I will rest. I look with wonder at people who don't worry or fret. How do they do that? How do they feel that sense of having a right to enjoy this moment? This is a very refined form of self-torture.

And yet like so many nasty little things, it has its advantages. I have become more modest in my desire for sensation. Two little pigeons sitting on my windowsill staring in at me give me moments of delight. They made their fleeting visit last spring, they tilted their heads to one side and regarded me with their shiny pebble eyes. I tittered because they reminded me of little head-scarved women, gossipy and curious.

'Now, Patricia, I have to say I think she's put on a bit of weight.'

'Hm, you could be right. Mind you, she was always a bit bottomy.'

Maybe that's what they were thinking. Probably not, but they were funny.

I think if I were content with my book, I would have missed the little nosey parkers. And that would have been a shame. So even when times are hard, and our dreams don't come true, if we can lower our expectations a little, life and Mother Nature will exchange a conspiratorial wink and lay before us little cabarets to amuse us.

I had to be satisfied with my pigeons and how they sparked my imagination, and I was satisfied until the next niggle wriggled in the pit of my stomach. Another trifle that causes more distress than it warrants because that's the way it is for me, for now. And if it means I can delight in gossipy pigeon ladies, then all is not lost, because all never is lost in the great scheme of things.

Please don't be ashamed of your tears. They are messengers from your marrow. There is something asking to be healed, and if you listen to your messengers and honour them, a way will appear to you. Part of it will be a way of the cross, but stay on the path and relief will come. Be intrigued by your sadness, it is a signpost to a better life.

When you feel the blackness inside of you, try not to look away, try not to run away, and please choose to stay alive. My blackness offered me a door and I opened it; the other side was still black, but in the way black velvet is black. When I really looked at it, it wasn't frightening, just lonely. When I sat with it, I didn't break, I just was. Try not to fear the blackness, just accept it and realise life can contain it and life can hold you. When you feel the blackness, try not to look away, try not to run away — and please choose to stay alive.

One morning last December, I woke up feeling
that now-familiar feeling. No hope, trapped, cursed,
that there will never be any dream-come-true.
Brushing my teeth was beyond me, getting dressed
was impossible. I schlepped to the kettle to make
coffee, stepping on my cat's tail in the process. She
screamed like a vampire and ran up the stairs, out
the window and down the avenue as if the hounds of
hell were behind her. I watched her progress. *Well*, I
thought to myself, *if I were you, puss, that's what I'd do too.*

Coffee in hand, I trundled back upstairs to my altar,
which is in a room with a glass door and a view of the
garden. There had been a light frost the previous
night, and what grass was left on the lawn looked like
a wedding veil. I was about to pray, churlishly, but I
would pray, when a slight movement in the garden
caught my eye. There, delicately emerging from the

shelter of the apple tree, was a little water hen. She tiptoed across the grass, picking as she went. Water hens are the pretty little aunts of the bird world, elegant, decorous and private. To see one is not rare but it is seldom. I watched as she tripped to the river, and silently floated away. Leaving nothing but the filigree of little feet in the frost.

I suddenly became aware of myself, I was smiling. My feathery fairy godmother had worked her magic. By this time my cat had come back; I turned to my altar and she hopped up on my lap. I began to pray.

I don't know how to do this, but I must. I must find strength within. I must find the part of me that can live with fear and loneliness and learn from it. Is it that we constantly move away from what we need to learn? I feel the temple within me. My ribs form the apse and the nave. And somewhere near the centre of my forehead is a stained-glass window. It is just a faint glimmer now. This is faith. To not know something is there but tend it nonetheless. I will pray now.

Love has reappeared. It was an ordinary tiff that
ordinary people have time after time, and it is
over. There was no need for drama. Again, I
suffered needlessly. Catastrophes galloped across
my imagination. My mind, the puppet master,
is stronger than my faith. My faith lives in that
expectant, untended temple. All roads lead there.
Life is the Way, but it is also the distraction.
I must not be distracted.

I prayed this morning. I asked for nothing, I said thank you. Thank you for the suffering. Thank you for the people. Thank you for the good and what I perceive to be bad. Everything I learn from being alive can be a torment or a light to hang in my dim inner temple. It is my choice. I like this insight, but, now, I have learned that pretty analogies are not the work. The work is harder, less poetic. So I step out the door to work. The mundane world where I must breathe my faith into life.

Self

Introduction

There is a 'self' and a 'Self'. The small *s* self is the
self of daily struggles, addictions and pain. The self
of fun and diversion and small comforts. The capital
S Self is the Self of connection, wisdom and love.
The Self of universality.

I think we travel through the struggles of the small
self and if we can process those struggles by taking
responsibility for our actions, we can expand and
grow to become a big Self that can encompass the
universe but can also be content to be as small as
the petals on a daisy.

Be small. Be nothing. Stop stirring. Be as small as a petal on a daisy, humming bird tiny. Be nothing as space is nothing, as air is nothing. Stop striving and fall back into the arms of the universe. This is how I have learned to rest. My head is the lap of infinity.

A wise Buddhist once said, 'This is how Buddhism works: if you're constipated and you're not chanting to have a great big poo, you're not practising correctly.'

To choose to be silly, to act the goat, the eejit, the
jinnet, the maggot, to give yourself over to inspired
buffoonery is very underrated. I want to discover
my hidden shallows, for too much depth can be
misleading.

Once after praying, I ran to himself and said,
'There is a big grin at the centre of the universe.'

I want to wear that grin, I want to guffaw like God.
To choose to be silly is to laugh at yourself — never
someone else, for humour can be cruel when
used as a weapon.

Silliness is a plastic hammer, not really practical but
delightfully absurd.

There is joy to be had in being bad at something.
I love to draw and paint, and I am a terrible artist.
I made one mistake, however. In an effort to be good,
I bought pencils and paints, enough to cover the
Sistine Chapel, and in the glut I cannot find what
I need. I need one pencil, soft and black, and I
need a blank white page. That is all. I must clear
the decks, find my pencil, make my mark and
enjoy my incompetence.

I have dreamed exotic dreams, of riches and glamour, of yachts and gowns and jewels, of villas that smelled of jasmine. I am preparing my lunch, a potato boils in a small pot, the searing bubbles turning the hard and inedible substance into food. No jasmine, no satin, just alchemy in an untidy kitchen. It is enough.

Let me open the lotus of my heart to include all
beings exactly as they are. Let me not judge or assess.
Let me have the grace to help when it's appropriate
and when it is not appropriate let me mind my
own bleedin' business.

A little round woman sat on a rock in Nice, in
the south of France. She could feel in the air the
presence of the things that delighted her. Lavender,
rosemary, lemon, olives, bougainvillea, wine.
The words – Côte d'Azur, Belle Époque, Riviera.
The people – Chagall, Matisse, Charles Trenet.
Beside her, families basked and toddlers toddled,
astonished at wet pebbles. Two lovers devoured
each other with dark eyes, turned over and offered
themselves to the sun. The Baie des Anges was bluer
than blue, so blue that it seemed the universe was
photoshopping itself. The little round woman lay
back and enjoyed the sound of the waves and the
crunch of the pebbles under the feet of the boys
selling Orangina.

Further down the coast, the Cannes Film Festival was
in full, glittering swing. Once the little round woman
dreamed of being there, her work admired, her body
lithe and encased in satin. Cinderella on a red carpet.
But, today, she sat on a rock on a beach in Nice.

The children squealed in delight, the parents gazed at the blueness, the lovers lolled in sultry-eyed indolence. 'Orangina, Orangina!'

Had this woman given up her dream of glamour? Oh no, life's not like that, dreams die hard, maybe they never die, for though all things must pass, all things are possible. Soon, she would leave the beach and stroll along the Promenade des Anglais. Take a kir and nibble almonds. But, for now, she enjoyed the symphony around her. The families, the lovers, the waves, the swooping gulls. A little round woman on a rock in Nice in the south of France.

There is a creature who lives in my brain and all she wants is to eat, read magazines and watch television. She is not interested in enlightenment, she likes to complain and she could bitch for Ireland. I dislike her intensely. She gets in the way of my aspirations and passions. I would like to see what she looks like. I would like to give her a piece of my mind. This morning, as I looked in the mirror, I thought I saw her but it was myself I saw.
I thought I heard her voice, it was faint, I thought it said, 'I am that which you do not love. Listen to me.' Her voice, though faint, sounded like mine. Of course, it couldn't have been, but it's strange, isn't it?

I have neglected my temple. Life and work have
distracted me. No lights have been lit of late but
those few brave candles are burning still. I have been
mistaken. I have seen the lights in yoga classes and
in front of altars but the sources of temple lights are
more varied. Now, I realise that the life and work
that distract me so are the greatest of all light sources.
It's easy to think that a farmhouse kitchen or a shed
or a theatre dressing room provide no spiritual
insight. They are not exotic, not mystical. They hide,
however, the richest lessons, they are places where we
are ourselves unadorned. The boredom, discomfort,
fear and guilt we often feel in ordinary life, in
ordinary places, are like Xs on a treasure map.
If we can stop and dig where we are, we may find
lanterns brighter than the stars.

Today I will do nothing. I will recognise my fatigue. I will sit and read, stretch and breathe. This is a new science for me, untried and frightening in its way. It must be done, however; I must meet myself, the stranger, in my own house.

Something is moving in my soul this morning.
I feel like wearing a cloak of fire and screaming.
I feel like being big, I feel that something is longing
to break fetters. Whenever I am truly myself, I feel
ashamed. I feel I must take back this self-hood,
disown it. Wherever I go, I try to fit in. To speak
the language, think the thoughts that keep me in my
place. The small place. I know, though, that what I
am is very big. Showy. Longing for expression.
I have left it to others to see this, but how can they?
My disguise is very thick. Do I have the guts to be
myself? It's strange to use the word 'guts', when to
keep myself hidden I stuff myself with food. It is
strange to use the word 'big' about my being when
only my body expresses this bigness. This is exciting,
clues are emerging. This day could be different ...

Was that day different? No. It was more the same than any day I can remember. I am disheartened. I thought insight would bring change. That, magically, I would now be different, serene, self-disciplined. Now I realise insight and change do not go hand in hand. Insight is like the architect's plan for a beautiful house, change is the back-breaking work of building it, brick by heavy brick.

The mind loves insight but hates change. That is why I sit each evening surrounded by sweet wrappers, my body heavy, my mind sugar addled, telling myself sure it's Christmas, I can start tomorrow, I've done it now; I might as well go the whole hog. I berate myself for having gone off track with my book. A book which was supposed to be about the little

things in life that are extraordinary, this book has
taken me down an unexpected path. Yet, actually, it
could not have been otherwise. I have been forced to
live with attention. If I see the outer world without
distraction then an inner journey must follow.
The two are inexorably joined. Ordinary beauty in
the physical world calls to the ordinary beauty of the
soul. Once the soul awakens, it will not rest until it
knows itself. Eating too much is not a cardinal sin,
there are worse addictions, but it is taking me away
from some essential learning. My path has always
been a spiritual one, so I carry on, an ordinary
woman with ordinary problems sitting in an
ordinary kitchen, seeking ordinary enlightenment.

I still want, desire, crave. Only in the morning am I
aware of the importance of my journey inside myself,
and the ordinary treasure it will yield. The treasure
of serenity. Of just here and now being enough.

I hold two entities inside me. One is a wise woman
sitting, with failing patience, waiting to be heard.
The other is an indulged, unhappy, unseen girl
who is drowning in all she has. As the day passes,
the quest for peace is forgotten in all the clamour of
life. I know I am getting close to the centre of myself
because the decoys are getting more devious and
stealthy. The desire for comfort, ease, the dreadful
weight of boredom tap me on the shoulder inviting
me to look away from the path. I must be vigilant.

Home Place

Introduction

I have lived all my life in the house I was born into.
The neighbours I know, but don't know, are there
constant and steady. 'Howiya, howiya.' The place-
names, memories and animals have a sense of refuge
about them.

But don't get too defined by 'home', for it can
stifle you. I feel at home in other places too, without
memories or personal history. The ridiculous blue
of the sea in the south of France cradles me in its
own way. In an immense universe, it's always good
to loosen the ties that bind.

The way my father put on his boots was fascinating
to me. I would sit at his feet and watch him every
morning. The trousers would be tucked into socks
and then he would take the left boot, loosen the laces,
insert his foot, tap the ground twice with his heel to
ensure a good fit. Then the lacing would begin.

Sometimes to humour me, he would unlace the
boots entirely and start the process from scratch.
I loved it when he did that. It was like a mantra in
movement over and back pushing the laces through
the little eyelets. 'We go in here and then we go here
and then we go arounnnnd there,' he would say,
to my delighted giggling.

When both boots were done, the laces firmly wound
twice at the ankle and tied in a double bow, he would
stand up, a giant in my eyes, and start the day's work.
I always felt safe in those days.

Sometimes I come home in the depths of night,
having driven from far away, sometimes north or
west, sometimes south or east. In the village, I take
the turn at the castle and that is my road home. I send
my prayer 'nam myoho renge kyo' down the chimneys
of the houses on the right and left as I go. I hope it
will explode with blessings on the hearthstones.

The little chair I sit on to pray is old and rough hewn. Many bodies have worn its seat smooth. It's no glossy Chippendale, having been made by humble peasant hands. It is secure. It holds me well, supporting my pleas to heaven.

Though it sits right in the middle of the Côte d'Azur and has all the allure of the south of France, I call Nice, Mullingar-By-The-Sea. For all its Belle Époque buildings, museums and art galleries, it is, at heart, a friendly market town. There is no self-conscious style, no yachts, no artificial beauty. Nice is a beautiful woman but a peasant woman, taking her ease by the sea, a basket of olives by her feet.

The progress of Jake (the dog)

7.30 a.m: Ooh, ooh, ooh, the door is opening!
There she is! Will I get the ball? No, I'll roll over.
No, I'll get the ball and then roll over. No, that won't
work, I'll roll over, she'll tickle my tummy, that's
nice. What's that? Is it John with the jeep? It's John
with the jeep, have to go, have to run, have to bark,
wheels won't go round unless I bark. Bark, bark! Up
to the field, must keep in front. Rabbit! Run after the
rabbit! Where'd it go? Where's John with the jeep?
Ooh, look, cow poo! Must roll in cow poo! Ahh,
that's great. Oh, John's out of the jeep. Must jump
up, to get my pet. What's this? No pet? Don't like
those words John says. It appears he doesn't like
to be covered in cow poo. People are weird.

9.30: Home again. I'll get the ball, John's giving
me doggy nuts, they're scrummy. Get the ball. John?
Where's John? What's that? Mick's tractor? Gotta go,
gotta bark. Bark, bark, bark, bark, bark, bark. There,
that's told him. My tail is up, my ears are pricked,
you don't mess with the Jakeinator. Where's John?
Oh, he's gone. Get the ball, she's going too. Oh,
well, a snooze in the hayshed.

11.00: Zzzzzzzzz

11.30: Zzzzzzz — what's that? Oh, it's the rooster. Zzzzzz.

12.30: She's back, get the ball. Way hay, she's throwing the ball. I'm in the gateway, she throws the ball, I catch. She laughs. Who's Packie Bonner?

2 pm: She's going off with those funny legs she has, the ones that go round and round. 'Bike' I think she calls them. Why does she need those legs? I'll go with her for a bit, as far as Fowler's house, he's the dog down the road. We don't get on. It's a long story. He barks but his humans don't let him out. Nice long widdle outside Fowler's house. Who's the daddy? Oh, he's getting out, run!

6 pm: Watching Jim feed the cattle. Oh, here she is. Get the ball. Oh no, time for bed. Still I'm hungry. She gives me a nice din dins. Roll over, she tickles my tummy. The door shuts. Where's the b— zzzzzzzzzzzzz.

**My name is Hetty. Hetty the hen. Pardon me if
I unburden myself.**

It's not that one minds, in fact it's not that one even
notices most of the time. Ben the rooster, he's really
quite a good husband, a good provider, always finding
little titbits for us, his little wives. A broken biscuit
here, a fat worm there, even some quite delicious
dog food. And we are grateful, Letty, Betty and I.
The thing is – and we all are in agreement over this
because we discussed it over a lovely drink of puddle
water the other day – that he is just too fond of his
conjugals. Now, as I said, it's not that we mind, and
it's true that we hardly notice his efforts, it's just quite
inconvenient. It's hard to get things done if he insists
on prancing around all the time. Letty's feathers are
in an awful state as he finds her particularly attractive

when she's preening. Actually none of us would mind
at all if he would just control himself during dinner.

There one is, picking at one's oats and whop!
Up he goes. Plays merry hell with the digestion.
We've tried talking to him, but he just cackles in what
he perceives to be a seductive way and says 'poussins
will be poussins'.

Bless him, though, he does have redeeming qualities;
if one looks very hard one finds them. Ooh, look!
A strawberry! Num num!

Oh, for goodness sake, here he comes. Just steady
myself. Five, four, three, two, one — finished. That
should keep him quiet till morning. Now, where's
that strawberry?

This is my religion. One day as I walked down the west pier in Dún Laoghaire, a seal bobbed up in the waters of the harbour. He was big and fat as butter, and he gazed at me placidly. To me, he looked like a character from Dickens, a maritime Micawber with his enormous moustache. *You funny old thing,* I thought. He blinked at me then slipped under the water. He did a sinuous somersault and faded into the murk. Just his tail was visible as, so gracefully, it undulated, silvery grey, and then disappeared. Comical no longer, he was a merman, holding all the legends of the ocean.

I love to travel, and I have so many beloved places.
A theme of my life for too many years has been
escape. I travelled to escape. I dreaded the home-
coming. Now, it is lovely to say that my most beloved
place is my own garden. It's not a prize winner, having
no flowers , but it has stones and ivy and trees and
breezes blow through bamboo all year round. I tie
prayer flags to the trees and stone Buddhas abound.
When I come up the drive having been away — in Nice
or Nenagh, Paris, Majorca or Mullingar — I get out
of my car, take a deep breath and become still. I look
up at my house and the sky above its roof and think,
it's good to be home.

In the evenings, as the light stretches, I go about my tasks. The final job of the day is the finding of the last hen. This little adventuress leads me a merry dance every day. She is the Freya Stark of the poultry world. She goes on treks, hikes and safaris. I stroll through the garden in search of her, my dog at my heels. I listen to the birds and sit on a bench to watch the dark, flowing river. In winter, I see the sun set or the moon rise and, in spring, my heart lightens at seeing new snowdrops. Summer and autumn have their magic too. The hidden buzz of insects on a July evening or the whoosh of crows' wings as they fly to roost in November.

Finally, the hen appears, sauntering up the garden, treating my chastising about lateness and foxes with insouciance. She knows she's not a nuisance but an instrument of the universe, she facilitates my Seeing.

There is a little river that flows outside my house.
It is brackish brown. It flows slowly, no babbling
brook, no Shannon glamour. But it has nourished
the land along its banks for thousands of years.
In dry times, it almost disappears but retains just
enough to slake the thirst of cattle. In times of flood,
the little river takes everything that's thrown at it.
A true friend. I must make my way down the
garden to say thank you.

Tommy always cut his cloth according to his measure.
As he aged, he placed objects in the right place.
Needing very little, he would have the turf placed at a
certain angle, the ash shovel just so. The sugar on the
table just there, the saucer on the sugar to ward off
flies. The spoon, it must be dry, placed in the mug.
He would eat ham and tomatoes for his tea. When
the floor was brushed, and the crumbs were gathered,
the table must be placed on the same lino squares.
He placed his chair in the sunshine but not where
the sun would blind. From this simple throne, he
would watch sparrows as they fought over the
crumbs from his table.

He knew how many birds there were.

The dog had been missing for five days. The man was broken-hearted. It was Easter week, and with hope almost gone, he went to a cathedral to pray. He bowed his head and said to the universe, 'Let him be there at the door when I go home.'

The man went home and the dog had not returned. So the man raised his eyes to the night sky. 'So be it,' he said.

Easter was early that year and snow fell upon his eyes. In the depths of night, the man was roused by a sound – something almost imperceptible – and he made his way to the source of the sound. He opened the door and there, in the snow, cold and bedraggled, sat the dog.

The man's handsome face was streaked with tears as he told this story, unembarrassed by his emotion. Soon, my tears joined his, I cried about the dog's return and because, I thought, maybe prayers are answered.

I remember a scene from my childhood. Two men,
friends — though they wouldn't say it — were cleaning
up the yard. They brushed the muck into piles and
then they worked together to put the piles into a
wheelbarrow to be brought to the dung hill.
They worked in harmony, one holding the shovel,
the other the yard brush. As the pile of muck
lessened, the shovel would be tipped this way and
that, the yard brush used deftly, to ensure that not
a speck was left ungathered. They never spoke
during the process, they seemed guided by an
inner choreography.

When they were finished, the yard was spotless.
A simple job well done can be a masterpiece.
I learned back then that sweeping muck can be
a meditation.

I love mysterious places. When I was a child, there
were so many. There was a little shop at the end of
the road where I lived. A lady called Katy owned
it. You could get your bull's eyes and chocolate,
the tea and the sugar, and ice creams, two-penny,
four-penny, six-penny. In Katy's house as you
entered the shop, there was a secret room — the
parlour. The door was always closed. It tantalised
me. I longed to see inside. Then one day, as I went
in for a liquorice toffee, the door was ajar. Katy was
still making her way to the shop from the kitchen,
I could see her through a little glass window in the
kitchen door. I sidled over, towards the half-open
portal to the chamber of mystery ... But Katy was
fleet-footed. She arrived before I could discern
what lay inside the room of secrets. I think I saw red
velvet and something gold in a cabinet. I bought my
toffee and left, Katy's watchful eyes seeing me from
the premises. It was good the little room remained
hidden from me, for the child I was thought I could
see Sheherazade draped on a couch.

I was looking for a darning needle. A rare thing.
In the back of the cupboard, I found the sewing box.
A biscuit tin. It wasn't rose-strewn and pretty, just
an old tin, scratched and forgotten. As a girl, I had
opened it many times, looking for pins and thread
to take up my latest pair of jeans. It meant nothing
to my young girl self. Now it was an Aladdin's cave of
memories. Thimbles, embroidery skeins, buttons,
buckles and fasteners all lay together giving time and
place to my past. My mother's nimble fingers were
the last to touch them. She was the age that I am
now. I want to say, 'I didn't know, Mum.' I didn't
know about the fear, the anxiety, the regret that you
must have felt, because now that I am ageing, I know
those feelings all too well. I don't blame myself for

my ignorance, for how could I know? But I can take responsibility. I can say, 'Mum, I will live for both of us.' I will be me until my dying breath. I will step out. I may not be able to leave behind these feelings that dog us both, but I will live with joy, as much as I can muster. Across time and space, I promise. With the threads of my past I will weave a present that has meaning. I cannot see the whole pattern of the cloth that I am weaving, it is too large and magnificent, but I will do my little corner as completely as I can.

Somewhere in that dim, untended temple, a candle sputters into light.

I woke up late today. I was grumpy, out of sorts.
I had my tasks to do and I didn't want to do them.
There is no such thing as leaving a farming task until
later, especially at the back end of the year when
daylight is scarce, so I made my way up the boreen
to count the cattle and sheep. I reached the highest
point on my land with grumbling bones aching.
The sun was low in the sky and shed a deep yellow
light. I could hear the wind in the Wolfs Wood, away
to the southwest, make its way to the Scots pines that
formed the boundary of the Asses Island, and then
it came to rustle the grass that lay golden at my feet.
Soon, I would turn for home, maybe I would leave
the boreen at 'Front of Mick's', go through Lovedice
Curragh and home by the Smoothen Iron, lulled by
the place names that surrounded me — I felt out of
sorts no more. I pulled my hood up over my head
and made for home.

Time Passing

Introduction

It is hard to age — but it is inevitable. If we could just stop and reassess our attitude to age and ageing, we could learn so much about the nature of life and the nature of contentment. I don't like ageing because I'm mouthy and opinionated, and I don't like being passed over. And let me tell you, Youth, the day will come when you will no longer be young and you, in turn, you will be pushed into the dimly lit corners of life.

Well, I ain't going anywhere. I don't want to be young again. I want to be who I am, what I am, the age I am. Just don't ignore me and, once in a while, ask me what I've learned.

Where do I belong?

I love clothes. I love style and originality. I love to
express myself through clothes. So far, so what?
Well, I commit a major sin every day and I am being
punished by the great god Fashion and the demi-god
Society. I have tried to rid myself of this appalling
sin — I have done penance, gone on pilgrimages,
I have even indulged in many refined forms of
self-flagellation. All to no avail. My sin clings to
me like a huge overgrown limpet.

What is this sin that so blights my life? I confess to
you my brothers and sisters, through my own most
grievous fault, I have aged.

I recently found a picture of myself taken when
I was in my early thirties. I was, I will admit,
shocked and saddened. When did this creature with
cheekbones, a jawline, a waist and, let's be honest,
an income, depart my life? When did the matronly,
wobbly-tummied hobbit I saw in the mirror this
morning arrive?

I try not to be ashamed of the hobbit, let's call her Lavinia Largebottom; after all, I'm encouraged to practise self-acceptance, self-love even, by the many well-intentioned self-help gurus whose books are causing my shelves to buckle. But, try as I might, I just can't bring myself to like Lavinia Largebottom. In fact, I would go so far as to say that nobody likes Lavinia or her many sisters. The fashion pack certainly would like her to take a hike to the nearest boot camp. Even if she returned from such a camp honed and lean, she would still have that age thing — and that will have her sent, likitty split, to the uncool step, where she would languish until she: (a) dies, (b) has to grab a Tena lady from her bag or (c) is proclaimed as a cultural icon because she is the only aged person in the universe with style.

It's a terrible wake-up call when you realise that you are now a member of the older generation. All the things I was so sure I was right about — fashion, language, music and all manner of popular culture — have changed so much that I now find myself disapproving of almost everything.

I disapprove of long dyed-blonde hair, pale lips
and those strange short dresses that look like
upside-down egg cups. I disapprove of people saying
'I done this, I done that'. People who say 'samwich'
drive me mental. And don't get me started on music.
When did wriggling and miming to the backing
track of a song that could have been written by a
chimpanzee pass for music?

Films I don't want to see include anything with an
actor barely over the age of consent saving the world
and lovey-dovey-they-hate-each-other-but-they-
really-love-each-other rom coms. Having 329
explosions or car chases that go on and on and on,
do not a film make, they an idiot make.

So where do I belong?

Where does a late middle-ager who doesn't want to be
biddable belong? I don't want to read about knitting
or grandchildren; if it weren't for Lavinia, I would
wear AllSaints clothes all day and I just don't care
for André Rieu.

Then, this morning, I turned on Sky Arts and there
she was, the answer to all my prayers. Chrissie Hynde
— sixty-two years of guitar-rocking, in-your-face,
what-are-you-looking-at woman. Then they all
started rushing into my mind. All those elders who
inspire not only their peers but anyone with a brain
— Patti Smith, Mary Robinson, Aung San Suu Kyi,
Debbie Harry, Helen Mirren, Leonard Cohen, the
Rolling Stones, Nelson Mandela, Joan Rivers — yes,
Joan Rivers — the Dalai Lama ... oh, I could go on.
What a tribe I belong to.

So let's stop putting people in the age box.
Whatever age you are, if you remain curious, engaged
and gently uncontrollable, there are new things to
learn, teach, discover and pass on. Every age has its
torments and its gifts. By George, I think I've just
inspired myself. I belong right where I am on this
planet, alive, vibrant and curious. So to hell with
boxes; I'm going to do what I want, wear what I want,
say what I want. Now where did I put my glasses?

I found a new line on my face today. It is just on the top of my lip. But it's not a disaster and I know I will get used to it. Age is making its presence felt and, in truth, I quite like it, but just for now, the sixteen-year-old who lives in my heart is inconsolable.

Not long after my mother had died, I went to her
grave. Back then, the little cemetery was surrounded
by open fields. I sat on the ground at my parents'
grave. I could see my beloved Lough Crew, navy blue
in the distance. To an onlooker, I must have seemed
bereft, a middle-aged, orphaned Buddhist, sitting
on the ground in a Catholic graveyard mourning
all who belonged to her. But in the earth that held
my parents' bodies, I felt a pulsing. The pulsing
of life and the thrust of it. From Lough Crew to
this Catholic place, to the allure of Buddhism:
a something that rejected nothing, that embraced
everything — life and death and our human struggle
to come to terms with what we don't understand.
I couldn't help feeling that nothing is lost in the
great scheme of things.

The warriors who catch my eye are those with sticks, walking frames and wheelchairs. Undaunted, they go forth, to live in this rushing world that is so hubris-dazzled that it hardly sees them. Hercules would be glad of such bravery.

They were old and sat together at the bar, staring
straight ahead. They drank slowly, not talking.
Unhappy? Maybe. Or maybe all those years
together had birthed a kind of harmony.
Maybe they accepted each other so perfectly that
sitting side by side was enough.

Love is not perfection. You loved my pretty, vibrant years and now as I slide ever further into the messy years, when the battle seems lost and I mourn times passing with bad grace, and become an out-of-sorts and dark-souled woman, you love me still.
How can this be? And yet it is.

That I can be unacceptable to myself and still be held by you. I have changed my mind. Maybe in this flawed and wobbly dance perfection lives, just wearing a disguise.

I don't like getting old. I mourn for my younger self, the power and vibrancy of her. She sat in the centre of her world, a world that saw and affirmed her. This older me has grown in body and shrunk in presence. She is largely ignored. Unless she screams very loudly, she is not listened to.

The worst thing we ageing people can do is go quietly. So I have decided I will be noisy, assertive and confrontational where necessary, until I go kicking and screaming from this life.

Firstly, I will look after my health, I will stay as fit and limber as my body allows me to. I will question at every hand's turn the values of this sleepwalking, youth-obsessed, unreal world. I will respect my anger, but I will not act on it when it is hot, I will leave it to cool like a newly made stiletto. I will not destroy with

it but rather use it to strip the excess from my life so
I can move lightly, wisdom's assassin, and take apart
piece by piece the hubris of those who disregard the
elders of our society. Because I have come to know,
as my years build up, that life is not about youth and
strength, it is a melding of youth and age, power and
vulnerability. One polarity needs the other. If I or
my peers go quietly, there will be nothing to soften
power, no one to guide and no one to shout stop
when the lemmings head for the cliff — they may
well still go over, but at least we will have tried.

Knitting is for old ladies. It's not edgy, it's not
fashion, it's not girly. Old ladies are just not edgy,
current or fashionable. They're just undesirable.

What do they do, those knitting old ladies?

Let me tell you what they don't do. In general,
they don't declare war. They don't make bombs —
well, maybe some might, but I'm sure they'd rather
not. They don't lie in wait to kick the daylights out
of someone. They rarely bitch and they live
modestly, not spending money on ridiculous
shoes they can't walk in, or handbags that look
like they were put through a shredder.
And they knit.

Usually clothes for other people.

Usually clothes to keep babies warm.

Being nosey, I study clotheslines. They are truly fascinating. In a strong wind they billow and snap. They are like conductors directing an orchestra of breezes. In stillness, they hang limp, like bats waiting for darkness. Shirts and blouses, skirts and trousers hang side by side. Babies' onesies and tiny T-shirts. And sheets, always sheets, the sails of life.

You can usually tell who lives in a house by its clothesline. A sassy young woman, should she be bothered, will hang out barely-theres. Barely-there thongs and barely-there bras, a silky chemise. A houseful of lads might treat you to a sleeping bag and a wetsuit. A raging cliché, I know, but never waste a good cliché. Then you have the young parents, rows and rows of tiny things, pink and blue, interspersed with exhausted tracksuit bottoms, and for older couples, bigger knickers and manly shirts, and pairs of socks rather than haphazard and lonely refugees, grey with overuse.

As life goes on, the clothesline diminishes again,
families part and spouses leave or die. The clothesline
now displays the gender-specific wardrobe of
perhaps an adventurous widow or the ordered man
on his own, in neat contentment. I don't find this
sad because it just means life goes on and has many
phases, and each phase has its meaning and purpose.
It must be lived and so many people live it so well.

But what strikes me most about clothes on a line
is their fragility. They are like us who wear them,
ordinary, lovely, mundane and heroic, blown and
buffeted, animated by that which we cannot see.

Dear Mary

I would love you to know that you are not ugly.
Please be kind to yourself. Hold on to that fight you
have in you, you will need it in later life. You feel that
you are strange because you don't think like other
people. Be patient, things *are* changing. Believe that
you will not always feel so controlled. The society that
tells you that you are wrong, and even sinful to want
to be free, will soon have very serious questions to
answer. It will be a while yet before that happens, so
please have faith in yourself and don't forget you're
not bad to think as you do.

Again, I remind you to keep fighting; this is so
important because I have a feeling your path is
interesting, but it is untrodden and it's not an
easy one.

Don't go on that diet! Oh, how I wish I could make
you see that you're just fine as you are.

Yes, men only want one thing – they can't help it,
they are wired that way. You, however, don't have to
give it to them. And while we're on the subject of sex,
sex is great; it is not a shameful thing and your body
is designed to give pleasure to yourself and others.
Freedom, however, does not mean being sexually
disrespectful to yourself or that you allow others to

disrespect you. Keep that thought in your head and cast out shame and enjoy your sensuality.

Please take ballet classes. You will really want to dance later on.

Go to Paris, you will love it. You will feel so free there.

Don't comfort yourself with food. Respect money. If you don't heed this advice, you will take a long and painful journey away from yourself and you will only start to find your way back in later years.

This is the way I think you should live your life but you have to learn from your own mistakes. Even if you ignore all that I have told you, you will still laugh a lot, love a lot and learn a lot. And you will always have your pesky curiosity about everything to keep you going.

But remember, keep fighting.

Lots of love

Mary

This is what my left knee taught me when one summer it chose to give me pain. It taught me I can't outrun my troubles. That I do violence to my body by thoughtlessness. So I sat and sometimes hobbled with my troubles on my shoulder. They didn't fade away, but they are not as heavy as I first thought. Now my knee works again, but I hold its lesson in my heart. The fire in my belly is still lit, I just move more slowly, that's all.

It's good to keep your dreams alive, just don't let
them take over. There is wonder here and now.
Keep your dreams alive, and surrender; surrender
is not giving in. It is falling back into the arms
of providence.

Like marriages, friendships go through different phases. I have had to learn this the hard way. There is the joined-at-the-hip passionate phase in youth. The ups, downs and chaos of puberty. Boyfriends, girlfriends, dizzy social lives. Then, when work and marriage and children come along, friendships often fracture. All my friends had children and I chose not to. I struggled to understand my place in their lives. The telephone didn't ring and nights out with my pals were few and far between. I labelled this as 'losing touch' and therefore losing friendship. The heart is not so petty, thank heaven: for all my hurt at losing status with my pals, I couldn't let them go. Now, as we all get older, we are coming full circle. Life is like that and we have to give those closest to us the right to live their lives, even their lives don't need us as much as we would like. I am letting go of my self-importance and picking up the pieces with my friends. We need our companions on the road of life.

Women

Introduction

Women aren't doing so well lately. Kidnapped, trafficked, underpaid — the twenty-first century has not delivered the freedoms and respect we deserve. In the West especially, we think we've done it, that the battle is won. We haven't. As long as women anywhere in the world are abused and treated with cruelty and contempt, we must keep fighting.

The women I write about here are strong, even in their pain. I love wild women, mad women, unbiddable hussies. So women, be bold and live your authentic life even if there is sadness in it. There are those who still long to be free; for these sisters and for those who have passed never having shone as brightly as they could have, let us be ourselves. Bold and strong and standing with our sisters.

Angelina Jolie's decision to have a double mastectomy was the talk of the planet. Many opinions have been given and experiences shared about the health of women. All the comment has got me thinking about our attitudes to our bodies, sexuality and where they sit in our consciousness when it comes to love.

Anyone who is in — or who has had — a loving, long-term relationship will tell you that in the beginning sex was the prime motivation for intimacy. So the physical attributes of the body seem to us to be a very important part of sexuality. As the relationship grows, you realise, however, that sexuality can be deeper and more soulful. Lovers' ageing bodies possess a sweetness and vulnerability which is endearing, but also sexually attractive.

It's a strange world when women with the cancer gene voluntarily give up their breasts for life, love and family, and yet other women voluntarily alter their breasts, making them unreal for ... well, for what? Usually it's issues of self-confidence, mostly based on feelings of lack of sexuality. But after the initial admiring glances, in terms of keeping a relationship with yourself and others going, those luscious prêt-à-porter breasts will leave you on your own.

I am sure Angelina Jolie would have given a lot not to have to do what she did, but it seems to me that her breasts do not define her, or her feelings of desirability. Her essence does that.

We are developing a 'physical appearance only' attitude to sexuality, and it's lamentably shallow. As women, we would, in particular, be so rewarded by care of our essence, our souls. By that, I don't mean saying three Hail Marys for purity, just that there should be a little less attention to cellulite and cup size, and a little more attention to our hearts, minds and emotional intelligence.

Soulful love is gritty and robust. Scars and damage don't faze it, it can see beyond perfect breasts, six packs and perfect limbs. It's tough, tender and deep, and it is also sexy.

Women who have had to lose breasts, who experience love and acceptance, know that they are still the vibrantly sexual creatures they have always been. They are wounded but nothing is lost. They have depths and strengths not defined by flawless bodies.

And, by the way, the Amazons, those fearless female warriors, were said to have cut off their left breasts so they could be better archers. That's not something I advise but, by goddess, I like their attitude.

While walking in Stephen's Green in Dublin, a woman passed me by. She was modestly dressed, a long skirt, kaftan and a head scarf. She smelled of musk and sandalwood. Her hips were large and luscious, and they swayed insouciantly as she made her progress towards Grafton Street, the pavement sizzling under her sandalled feet. I watched her, almost startled by the strength of her sexuality. Men, poor things, who hoped not to sin when they looked at her, what chance did they have?

The Virgin Mary speaks

Whose idea was this? What eejit thinks that I want to
be the poster girl for no fun? The sex thing doesn't
bother me – quite frankly I prefer whist – but all this
standing on serpents and looking up to heaven lark
just isn't me. I didn't want this, your Man didn't want
this, so who in heaven's name thought it up? My bet
is on a human who decided one day, 'I know exactly
what God wants. Loads of suffering, lots of rectitude
and a virgin mother.' What a load of old cobblers.

As you have probably guessed, I am not a willing
serpent standing-oner – and why a virgin? As if
bits of bodies are shameful. They're not, you know.
Bodies are great – all right they get creaky and old
and sick sometimes (soul eternal, body mortal, a bit
of a design flaw, bear with us, we're working on it)
but bodies are to be enjoyed and revelled in.
So drop the shame.

While I'm on the subject, having sex willy-nilly and just being plain vulgar is as much a pain in the bottom for me as the three 'Hail Mes' for purity. Because purity really isn't about sex or no sex. You can think what you like because we gave you free will, more's the pity, but I think purity is about respect, for yourself and for others, and, don't quote me, but I think you can have sex without love and still be pure – as long as you have respect, as long as you have 'like'. Don't treat one another like sex toys, just have a nice time.

Do you get me?

So there you have it. So, now, please could someone paint a picture of me in a wetsuit surfing in Bundoran?

To all you fashionistas, may I suggest you buy a Goofy hat. The one with the long ears. Keep it beside your mirror. And when you've primped and preened, before you go out into the world, put it on and take a good look.

I tell you this because I have lost years of my life fretting about my appearance. Then, I was given a Kermit the Frog hat as a theatre opening-night present. After the show I dressed in silk and wore earrings that sparkled in the light. I put on Kermit and looked in the mirror. Did I look silly! I took the frog from my head and left my dressing room to meet the public; the smile on my face and the giggle in my heart took years off me. Silliness is cheaper than Crème de la Mer.

What joy it is to gather twigs in the evening. There is a full moon and the light lasts longer. I bend and dip between the trunks of trees. A character from a mediaeval tale. Thank heaven they no longer burn witches.

There is a woman I know who lives at the base of a
magic mountain and she dances all the time.
She capers around the kitchen to jigs and reels, and
sways to laments. She dances with the seasons too.
She varies the steps to the passing of time. The light
skip of spring as she plants the peas and beans, she
spins to the Viennese waltz of high summer, in
autumn it is a mazurka as she sinks her long, slim
fingers into the earth to pull out beets. In winter,
she rests, her toes towards the glowing embers,
but still those toes twitch with the pulse of life.

I know another woman who dances all the time. She is lean and tough. Her hair is long and glossy. She makes her way through the streets of Paris every day, down Rue de Savoie, to the bridge at Saint Michel, she doesn't stop to take in the beauty of the Seine. For she must dance. She looks straight ahead, for she must dance. She passes Hôtel de Ville in winter, not seeing the whirling skaters on the rink outside its door. For she must dance. As Notre Dame strikes seven, she melts into the Marais and disappears from the street into the courtyard of the dance school. There, she spins and pirouettes, her long arms *en attitude* above her head. This is the second, perhaps the third ballet class of the day. For she must dance, this lean, tough woman.

I met her father once. He had a number tattooed on his arm.

He had spent four years in Auschwitz.

On the way to get Mammy dinner in Mullingar,
I stopped to buy a paper. And there she was at the
shop counter, counting change to buy her son some
sweets, Helen of Troy. Sallow skin, pale green eyes,
a bewitching profile. I couldn't help myself. 'Do you
know how beautiful you are?' I asked her. She threw
her head back and laughed, her white teeth beaming.
'Yes,' she said gently. I'm glad she knew. I went
my way hoping she never left Sparta.

I like witches. As a child, I always wanted to be one.
I never understood the allure of the fairy, unless she
was a bold one. I think that child I was, full of drive
and questions, felt drawn to witches because of their
power. They were women and they were listened to.
That didn't happen in the world that I grew up in.
Now without sabbats and brooms, I live the life of a
witch. Often alone and sometimes lonely. My hands
are dirty and my fingernails torn. I live under skies
full of hawks and on earth full of hares. The wind in
November trees thrills me. I don't like pink unless it
is the pink of dawn. Black, mysterious and vibrant,
not evil or sad, is the colour of my soul. I am no
longer a child full of impotent power but a woman
who questions and doesn't care. A wagon, a hayro,
a heart scald, a witch.

Beauty

Introduction

I need beauty. I think everybody needs beauty.
In this section, I write about soul beauty. Innocent
vanity, the vanity of a child who loves her party dress.

The beauty of nature regularly floors me. I wish
I could learn the modest lesson of an orange blossom
that blooms just because it can. I am a bit more
corpulent than that sinuous blossom, but I like to
adorn myself: perfume in the haggard, lipstick
with the cattle.

I also love the beauty of people, flawed human
beauty, without nips and tucks, the richness of a life
in a face and body. The beauty of human fragility.

I am obsessed with inner life to the extent that I sometimes lose sight of the outer layer. We have bodies, and sometimes we forget them or, in many cases, grow to hate them.

I have fought with my body all my life, I have hated it and punished it, and still it agrees to carry me around. It's about time I started to appreciate it, cosset it and maybe even decorate it, and I invite you to do the same. Maybe some of the actions here might not be for the lads ... but, then, who am I to say?

I bought a fur coat last week. It is sleek and shiny
and it hangs in my bedroom. I love to look at it and
all its iconic glamour. When I put it on, I run my
fingers over its shallow, hard surface. Then its
beauty increases. It isn't real.

I wonder if I ever told my mother she was beautiful. I hope I did. Because she was, and I don't think she knew it. She may have wondered while putting on her lipstick, but I'm sure she would have put such notions from her head. Because that's what you did in those days. It's a pity when beauty goes unsung. Tell someone they are beautiful. Don't leave them to wonder. Late as it may be, I will say it now: My mother was a beauty.

Some years ago, I played Maggie in *Dancing at Lughnasa* in Manchester. Every night, my friend and I would walk home through nightclub alley. Every doorway of every club and every pub boomed with drum and bass, people screamed at each other in an effort to communicate. By the time I got back to the flat in which we lived, I was anxious and enervated. I would close the door and breathe out.

However, some nights I would 'go out' after the show, which meant I was on the streets as the crowds poured into the nightclubs. Having led a sheltered life as far as clubbing was concerned, I found the accepted dress code for girls deeply shocking. I feel like a horrible tut-tutter when I say that. However, I remember the world when women had to scratch and fight for even the smallest freedom and, yes, we wanted the freedom to dress and express ourselves as we saw fit — but with the proviso that we kept our brains in gear.

Wearing thongs as outer wear, dry humping and throwing up in the gutter is not expression of freedom, it is a journey away from the self. It is saying, 'I am only my body and its wants. My physical self is the only reality.' It is saying, 'Take me.' I don't believe that women deserve what they get if they dress provocatively, but those nights on the streets made me so sad.

Then one Saturday morning in Kendals, the grand old shop of Manchester, I was trawling through the designer department (my journey away from self). I was served by a beautiful Muslim girl wearing a hijab. No doormat she, no enforced docility, she had a passion for style and colour and she was damn good at her job. She had dignity and grace and she knew who she was. And this feminist Mary McEvoy, who had heretofore abhorred forced modesty, began to think about modesty as a weapon, not a shield. I am sure that young Muslim woman chose her weapon, the hijab, and I salute her.

The burqa. We don't like it in the West. Because women don't have to hide themselves in the West, do they? They are free, aren't they? Because nobody tells us what to do. We love our clothes, don't we? And we like to look nice. So we wear lots of makeup and it's not because we're afraid of our faces being real. Because our society tells us the natural look is in, it doesn't matter what you look like. Fat or thin, no pressure. Ageing, great, bring it on. Cellulite is great — yes, you can have cellulite and we'll still think your bikini-clad, post-baby body is smokin' hot. Oh, yes, we love our women in the West. In the West, our women are so free. I mean, look at our celebrities — so natural, so happy in their skins, true role models.

We never judge our women, we love them no matter what and we protect them.

Yes it's great to be a modern woman. Equal pay, equal representation, total control over our own lives.

So we dress up and we go out looking like the free hot mamas we are. Makeup, false eyelashes, hair extensions, shellac nails, maybe a bit of Botox (naughty), Spanx, push-up bras, skyscraper shoes and if we want a tummy tuck we'll have it because we really like ourselves. We are free women of the West, thank God we never have to wear a burqa.

While searching for the perfect green leaves to put on my altar, I met the orange blossom. It was a slender branch hanging low over the ground. The white flowers, four petals perfectly arranged, the stamens like a buttery diamond, were placed along the drooping branch with an artistry no human being could effect. In that moment, it's simple elegance took my breath away. 'Oh, you're so lovely,' I whispered. At that, a soft breeze animated the branch and it swayed back and forth like a temple dancer.

Maybe it's my madness but, in that instance, it seemed that the orange blossom had responded to my wonder. As if my compliment had warranted a response. If it spoke, what would it have said? 'Oh, this old thing? I've had it for ages.' Would it blush and mumble an embarrassed thank you? Would it bask in the glow of my admiration?

I'm glad it's an orange blossom because its response was silence save for the whoosh of the little breeze, but my madness says it would say, 'I know my beauty but I am not proud. It is what I am in this eternal moment. And I am glad I gave you such delight.'

Over breakfast one morning in Ennis the men
sat at their tables; the golf had been good and the
hangovers seemed to be absent. I declared to myself
that I was surprised. I thought that, being a wise
observer of the world, I knew the score. Weekend
away, bit of golf, more than a few pints, a bit of a
lech, nudge nudge – you know yourself.

But, no. Breakfast was a relaxed affair. No guffaws,
no 'jaysus the state of you'. Just gentle chat. *Well,
well, I got it wrong*, I thought to myself, disappointed
in the lack of cliché. And then the beauty arrived.
Tall and slim, she flowed into the room. Gleaming
hair, perfect skin. She walked with the knowledge of
the effect she created and I marvelled that so much
physical perfection could come to rest in one place.
I waited. *Here we go*, I thought to myself. And I waited
for the leers to come, waited for the eyes to follow her
progress. 'Would you look at that.'

The beauty got her breakfast and sat ramrod straight
at a table in the middle of the room. Beside the men.
She was reserved, almost frosty.

'So, where are you from?'

Ah, the old chestnut.

'Dallas, Texas.'

'My brother lives in Galveston. Lovely town.'

And that was it. The men returned to their chat and the beauty ate quietly. Rapunzel without her tower. She left soon after, unnoticed by anyone.

Except me.

Let me try to love my body as it is. I have rejected it for so long — it was never good enough. My poor old ordinary body. It has carried me and tolerated my mistreatment for so long. So, I want to apologise to my hips and my thighs, my belly and my arms, my kidneys and colon, my liver and brain. I am sorry I never see the miracle you are. And if you forgive me, I will make amends and grow to love you and care for you. My ordinary body.

For all my desire for simplicity, I love glamour,
the glamour of a 1930s screen goddess, all dark,
shiny eyelids, and satiny hips. So, sometimes, I wear
red lipstick with my wax jacket. Jean Harlow of the
hay bales. I sashay to herd the cattle.

One day last year, I bought new perfume; its bottle
was an ornate vial. Smooth and glittering, it could
have graced a shelf in Byzantium, an alchemist's
shelf perhaps, full of shadows and mystery.
The scent was amber and sandalwood, frankincense
and musk. I dabbed it behind my ears as I went to
check my sheep. Empress Theodora walked with
me in the haggard.

Today on a train in Paris, I saw a beautiful human being. He was tall and slender and black as night. Black dreadlocks tied back, obsidian eyes, black coat. He sat almost decorously, his elegant hands joined on his lap. He wore thin gold bracelets, one on each wrist, silver rings sparkled on his fingers and on his coat, gold buttons. I wanted to stare and stare — not lasciviously, he seemed above all that. A fine-boned ebony prince. Do I seem over the top? You didn't see him. The train was late, people around him complained, he smiled and said, 'Oh, it's just normal.' His smile was gentle, his voice soft, his accent, probably African, I don't know. I wonder how many times he has been told to go back to his own country? I hope he stays.

Community

Introduction

Over the years, I have been in different communities.
The free-wheeling, irreverent community of the
strolling player; the down-to-earth, no-messing
community of farming; and the confused and
lovely community of the mentally distressed. Add
to this, the Buddhist community, the belly-dancing
community (no kidding), the tennis community,
the running community ...

We create communities around us all the time.
And we lose them too. The only community that we
all belong to at the same time is the those-who-are-
alive community.

I love to observe my fellow human beings going
about their lives. I value my connection with them
and when I feel connected to Life, a junkie is my
teacher and my brother. I value small treasures, like a
fire that has been set for me on a cold morning, and
I see the sacred in a shared path with my neighbour.

Sometimes I have had to sever connections; this is painful. Usually, it has been out of a sense of self-preservation, when I don't know how to protect myself from a friend's behaviour. I don't know if my decision to end a friendship is correct or not, so I get in front of my altar and chant for their happiness and good fortune, and resolve to love them from afar, in that place where egos can't create strife.

Now that I think of it, it pays to fall out with me!

My guardian angels wear woolly hats and wellingtons.
They set fires, feed cattle and carry heavy things.
They are a far better kind of angel than those wafty
heavenly beings — besides, those wings would never
fit in the cab of a Massey Ferguson.

One September day on Dublin's Wood Quay, I came
across a distressed man. He seemed to dance on the
spot, bending forward and then stumbling back.
The dancer was very near the edge of the pavement
and in danger of weaving into the traffic. I asked
him what was wrong. He stared at the ground and
mumbled incoherently. I looked down and saw that
the lace on his shoe was undone. He had been trying
to tie his lace, but the heroin that coursed through
him meant that he did a joyless dance instead.
I knelt before him and tied the lace. Soon tears
came to my eyes as I realised I was not really tying
a junkie's lace, but paying homage to a saint who
drew such kindness from me.

A woman I know embraces silliness with such
gusto that she sweeps me along, often helpless with
giggling, in her wake. Her portfolio of eejiting
includes: arriving at a very posh hotel to meet two
glamorous friends in a fright wig, joke teeth, and
a long and very shabby skirt streeling along behind
her; a slimming club in a cattle trailer complete
with scales, stethoscope, a cattle prod for aerobics
class and a garden hose should her clientele desire a
colonic; careening around boreens at 20 mph on a
little scooter, Meatloaf blaring 'Bat out of Hell' from
speakers, with some helpless guffawing creature on
the back, begging her to cease the tomfoolery
but not really meaning it.

To call her on the phone is to gift yourself with a
surreal monologue that leaves you begging for mercy,
because the old ribs can't take it any more. It's so
joyous to be swept away like that. I think the Dalai
Lama would approve of my friend's spiritual (in)
discipline, for ego and vanity are helpless before it.

Taking coffee in the city on Sunday morning is
a delight. People amble, unhurried. I have my
favourite coffee shop. I know the Ukrainian lady
who gives me my latte, she calls me darling. And she
dances as she bakes, brioches and croissants and such
cakes, oh! Chocolate and coffee and berry and cream.
She says she dances love into her work. That is true,
for I have felt it.

On this cold mid-morning in October, the month
of my birth, I realise my wants are insatiable but my
needs are few. Just comfort, warmth and ease
of mind.

In my troubled head, comfort and ease of mind seem
out of reach but, in the hearth, some wood gathered
by a good friend lies waiting; I hunker down and
strike a match.

It was a so-so morning. I was driving along the quays
to work. On the radio, the same voices — mostly male,
it has to be said — talked the same talk about money
and the economy and power and what we should do.
As if anyone really knew. The traffic lurched along
like an injured caterpillar and I was bored. I turned
off the radio and looked for entertainment on the
street. The car was motionless, needless to say.
The street didn't disappoint. Outside a church,
I spotted an unusual sight. A garda in uniform
hunkering down to a baby buggy as the parents
watched on. The traffic moved a little and as I drew
nearer, I could see that the uniform held a ban garda,
round-faced and smiling. She was tickling the baby's
soft, round tummy. Her head wriggled from side
to side. I couldn't hear, but the motion was that
familiar one that's made. 'Who's a lovely baby?
You are. Yes, you are.'

The guard stood up, still regarding the infant. Her
eyes were shining. Was it her first day back at work?
Did she yearn for her own baby, at home without her
for the first time? Or was she hoping one day that she
would notice the belt of her uniform getting tighter
and smile secretly to herself?

The scene ended quickly. As if some inner policing radar kicked in and she was now as alert as a prowling leopard, her head turned to watch the traffic. The smile was gone, the eyes were now steely. I saw what she had spotted. A chancer in a shiny Rover was sailing blithely down the bus lane. Her hand went up. *Here we go*, I thought, *she'll pull him over*.
But, no, like a kindergarten teacher, she put him in his place. Get in lane, you bold boy, and the motorist immediately complied. She was a practical woman; the traffic was bad enough, name taking and summonses would only make it worse, so she fixed the problem and let it go.

The scene ended as she sauntered down the quays. I turned on the radio again, the voices burbled on. I suddenly wanted to run after the guard and ask her how she would fix the world.

I met my neighbour one September evening,
coming down the road with his cows as I was going
up. The path we trod was gravelly with large stones
worn smooth by the feet of his family and mine, his
animals and mine. His stick, which he carried in his
surprisingly elegant hands, was also smooth through
many years of use. He is a frugal man. We passed the
time of day, and chatted a little about his cows,
serene and sleek.

As always, I wanted to say, 'I admire you and your
unerring sense of self. I am so fond of you.' I kept it
to myself because you keep those things to yourself
where I come from. We parted, he to his home to
tend his cows, and I carried on, the path that he
had come down, a sacred way.

We have parted. Our friendship is spent, even shattered. So sad that it came to this. But I have learned a lot. I have learned that what you believe about me is not my truth — but it is yours, so it is truth for you. Your nails are long and red, and you scratched me hard, but only my good-girl vanity. So go your way, shake your tail feathers and live a wonderful life. When all is said and done, our deepest selves understand that darkness cannot smother love.

I go to Paris whenever I can. I remember the first
time I went there I cried because every cliché was
true. The smells, the energy, the cafés, the people,
the magnificence. I did the tourist thing — the Eiffel
Tower, the *Mona Lisa*, Notre Dame — but the Paris
moment I treasure most happened not long ago.
I had been out for a run along the, by now familiar,
banks of the Seine. It was very cold, so I popped
into a modest little café on the Île Saint-Louis
for a coffee.

'Bonjour, Madame!'

'Bonjour, Monsieur. Une noisette, s'il vous plait.'

I stood at the counter with my coffee, no one looked
up, the man beside me read his paper. Coffee
finished. 'Merci, Monsieur!'

'Merci, Madame.'

I went out into the cold, completely happy.
By the hokey, I thought to myself. *I'm a local.*

I had plans today. I would write the book, break the back of it, then I would count the cattle and sheep. I would then feed the lambs and chickens. If my friend was free I would ask her to meet me for coffee. Then maybe I would buy a wheelbarrow, because I need one badly. Would I go to a yoga class this evening? Yes, that would be a good thing to do.

Then at ten to ten, I heard my neighbour had died. I have spent the past hour staring at the wall.

He is gone from them, his strong wife and children.
Brave eyes weep. Big men cry. We sit in the kitchen,
neighbours not knowing what to say. So we say
nothing. Cups of tea are handed round. A man
stares at the table running his fingers over the edges.
Ringtones puncture the silence.

'Yes he is, about an hour ago. I know, and thanks
for calling.'

And eyes well up again.

I don't know how to bear them up, so I take my leave.
As I leave the house, I see his daughter, strong and
straight, returning, bucket in hand from feeding
cattle. She walks on the track he made on the grass.
A fitting tribute.

I will now pray for him. It's the only thing for me to do. A wise man once said that the opposite of death is birth. That life has no opposite, so I will pray for life to carry him and his grieving clan to the other side of pain.

The woman was about to lose her home. For weeks, her face was strained with worry, tears flowing no matter how hard she tried to stop them. Then, one day, two fairy godmothers appeared, waved their wands and magicked her away. They took her on a Viking boat, a silly tourist boat on wheels that barrelled through the streets of Nordic Dublin. The godmothers waved their wands again and conjured up three plastic Viking helmets. First, the fairies put them on and then they crowned the sad woman with silliness. Off they went on that ridiculous boat, laughing magic laughter. When the odyssey was over, the woman couldn't cry any more – she didn't want to cry, she had used up all her tears in mirth.

Please know the truest, most valuable things in life
don't come with fireworks. They are shy. They come
wrapped in breezes, warm and cold. They can be
tasted, felt, seen and touched. They are stealthy.
Remember to stay alert.

Today, myself and two neighbours put ourselves
out to find my dog's favourite toy. A filthy old tooth-
marked ball. He had let it roll into the ditch in front
of my neighbour's house. My neighbour's crooked
stick was found and my herding stick was also deemed
to be a useful tool. So there we were, me on my knees
with the crooked stick and my neighbour's pretty
niece with my stick manoeuvring gingerly the scuffy
ball from the ditch while my dog looked on in grave
concern. His ears pricked in concentration as his
treasure came ever closer. Soon, the silliness of our
task became apparent but we continued on through
fits of giggles. Soon, the ball was in the dog's mouth
and I went my way, smiling. It was a delightful way
to spend time; I like knowing people who do
such things.

Nature

Introduction

Nature means everything to me. More than anything else, it is my religion. If I were to preach in this book, I would say: 'Be modest. Don't try to dominate your natural environment. Respect it, and fall in love with it and all its creatures. Learn about how it works and adapt to its behaviour. Let your humanity be a loving cog in the wheel of creation, not a blight on it. You will be happier, I promise.'

Make this the first thing you do. Go outside in the morning — rain or shine, wind or cold. Take a few breaths and feel the enormity of the universe.
I gently suggest you put out your hands, palms up, and no matter what is happening in your life, even if it seems unbearable, say thank you. It will make sense, I promise you.

Every little thing contains a miracle. The eye of a thrush, the shyness of a narcissus, the dizzying variety of grass heads. Appreciate spectacle, but don't let it dazzle you because you could miss the little things. And little things yield magic too.

I had forgotten how beautiful this place – Deià in Majorca – is. Full of sun and leaves and mountain, the sea just on the horizon. This morning on my way to the village, winding my way through the flowered – all wild – lanes, I heard whistling, a soaring kind of whistling and a beautiful melody which changed to singing, rasping and throaty-voiced. I looked around to see the owner of this wild song. The lane was empty, save for a sleeping cat under a bamboo bush. 'Well, puss, lovely as you are and crazy as I can be, I know it wasn't you.'

The whistling began again and I noticed another bamboo quiver to my left. The sound came from a small, overgrown gully. I looked down and could see nothing but shaking bamboo and purple flowers. The whistling continued. It was so pleasing I wanted to capture it, so I took out my iPhone and pressed

record. The whistling stopped soon and a lean,
pony-tailed young man emerged from the gully
into a garden on the other side. He was the Whistler
of Deià. A gardener clearing away summer's dying
leaves. '¿Qué tal?' he shouted to a mate, as he trotted
across the forecourt of the house whose garden he
was tending. He was mortal after all. No gypsy
phantom. I went about my business.

Later that day, I listened back to my I phone:
33.4 seconds was all I had of the whistler. Like
summer's leaves on that October day, I would
have to let him go.

I can almost see Lough Crew from my house. It is
twenty miles away to the northeast in Meath. I love
its distant roundness. It is a megalithic site. High
majestic cairns strewn with spiralled stones
and chambers.

I have always longed for sacred ground, and Lough
Crew has all the glamour of the past. A past when
people knew they lived in mystery. Our modern
world, for all its knowledge, can tell us nothing new
about who we are. I climb Lough Crew many times
a year. Usually on Celtic feast days — Bealtaine,
Lughnasa, Imbolc. I go there to unknow.

There is a tree in Nice and it's a friend of mine,
it's right on top of the citadel overlooking the city.
It is a pine tree and not remarkable, but I love the
sturdy green of its boughs against that bluest of skies.
I visit the tree whenever I can, it reminds me of
the day I first saw it, when it did what friends do.
It made me smile.

I went to see the Alhambra once. The Moorish palace
in Granada. I had read of its beauty many times, and
friends who had seen it were ecstatic. It was indeed
lovely, room after room of ornate marble carving.
Cool, dark vestibules and tinkling fountains. But
my favourite part was a courtyard with a rectangular
pool. Clear and still. Swallows had nested in the
walls around the pool and their darting images
flashed across the surface of the water. I sat by the
pool a while. Now, years later, when I think of the
Alhambra, all I really remember are the swallows.

It was a hard winter's night. In my car, it said
nine below. It had snowed that day and frost had
made the road crackle as I drove across the bog on
a lonely road. The bog stretched out each side of
me to infinity. The snow was blinding white and it
reflected what moonlight there was. I had a Leonard
Cohen CD in the car. I stopped and rolled down
the windows and played 'Hallelujah', loudly to the
emptiness. It seemed the right thing to do.

It is spring. A time of optimism. But, please, not
Pollyanna optimism because life contains darkness,
it cannot be otherwise, so don't wish it away. Even the
daffodils, so cheerfully yellow, lived in the old black
earth; its hard frostiness bruised their tender shoots
but still they dance in the harsh March winds.

The clocks went forward last night, and as I fed
the sheep this morning in the early hour, the world
was still. No cars, no human voice, just the spring
— warm breeze and cooing pigeons. Co coo coo coo
coo, the whole world's watching, the whole world's
watching. The sky was low and leaden, but laden with
spring. Later, while having breakfast, I turned on the
television. 'Buy now!' 'Get this!' 'You deserve this!'
Business, the economy, technology. I looked at
the velvet sky and switched off the cacophony
of nonsense.

Little fungi that seem so inconsequential are
powerhouses of change. Their essence creates soil,
which grows plants, the plants, in turn, feed animals,
and both animals and plants feed human beings.
And so we live in our vainglorious power unaware
that so little a thing has created our sustenance.

So, go to the woods, find the tiniest toadstool, join
your hands at your chest, just where your lungs
breathe in and out, and bow to your benefactor.

I began this book at Samhain, just heading into winter. It is now February. It is evening and the days are lengthening. I am walking along the boreen that runs past my house. It is wild and it is cold. The country has been battered by storms; homes, fields and shops lie in water. It is a time of hardship for many. I stop and listen. High in the bare, swaying trees, Hope lives in throats of birds.

Ohhhh my God, it's freezing! That's the battle cry
of the Forty Foot, the gentlemen's bathing place on
Dublin Bay. And, yes, it is James Joyce's Forty Foot
and, yes, gentle ladies now swim there too. Even
on the warmest of days it is bracing. The swimmers
make their way down the seaweedy steps, the brave
plunge in and the timid, like myself, go gingerly,
dreading every shrieking step. Eventually there is no
going back and in you go, your breath goes, and you
swim like the clappers, out, out, out. Sometimes a
seasoned swimmer, usually over seventy, will pass you
at a leisurely pace, like a seal in no particular hurry.
'Lovely today,' they might say. You resist the expletive
that is hovering over your tongue and chatter 'a
b-b-bit cold' instead, but Poseidon has gone out
of hearing round the corner on his way to Sandycove.
You turn for home, by this time your body has
acclimatised to the sea. And you glide through those
nurturing waves to the steps and you realise, yes, yes,
yes, it is lovely today.

I went to herd the animals on Christmas Day. It was a sunny, sharp day and frost lay untouched on the floor of the wood I planted. The trees were getting up well. Oak and alder and larch. Birches stood out against the piercing blue skies. I sat on a rock in my field, looking at my wood – the one that I had planted – flourishing on that pale-blue day, and I marvelled at my wisdom.

Cosmos

Introduction

And so we return to the beginning. This section is called 'Cosmos'. In the introduction to the book, I wrote about a Buddhist phrase: 'No affairs of life or work are separate from the ultimate reality.' I think we miss so much when we try to get somewhere else – be it physically, emotionally or spiritually – when all the time, treasures simple and grand are unfolding all around us. To see them is to be blessed.

Keys are sacred objects. I mean ordinary keys ... car keys, door keys, the keys we lose umpteen times a day. They are instruments that cause insanity if we live in our addled heads. We distractedly fling them here and there and give ourselves everything from heartburn to heart attacks when we can't find them. But if we use them correctly, they are tools for spiritual awakening.

To be present in the now is the building block of enlightenment, so the next time you have your keys in your hand, come into present time, not thinking or fretting or worrying, just Here, with your keys in your hand. Take in how good it is to stop and just Be. Then in that advanced spiritual state, put them away. When you need them again, you will remember where they are. Which is a very desirable side-effect to being at one with the cosmos. Who would have thought it? The door to the Micra and to nirvana open with the same key.

In the evening go outside; this time raise your hands, arms outstretched, over your head, join your hands and bring them to the front of your heart. Bow your head. Even if this doesn't make sense — maybe *because* it doesn't make sense — try to do it. It's good to be humble once in a while.

One evening on my holidays, a fly flew into a
sunbeam. It was a late-evening sunbeam, golden and
intense, and it lit the fly's tiny wings, giving them a
buttery iridescence. Now, even by fly standards, this
fella was minuscule. A bluebottle would have King
Kong proportions compared to him. The light on his
wings was entrancing and he stood out wonderfully
against dark green, evening leaves. I thought to
myself, *My God, what size is your little heart? Do you have a liver,
kidneys, intestines?* Can you imagine anything as tiny as a
fly's intestines? The wings fluttered how many times
a second? *How long do you live, little fly? What kind of life is it,
in all this space, surrounded by swooping swallows and humans who
swat with abandon? And yet you hover in sunlight, driven to live.*
A microscopic universe.

In the sky above, stars would soon come out. Stars
that stretched across constellations and galaxies, and
into infinity. And here was I, sitting on a balcony

in Deià, Majorca. Did the universe regard me as I regarded the fly? Tiny, minuscule, insignificant? My heart so tiny.

All my worries and vanities must be almost laughable to such immensity. But small as the fly was, I was entranced by the beauty of its sunlit wings. Its drive to live in adversity. It lived just to live, it was content to be a fly. I hope one day that I will live content to be who I am, just a tiny thing in the universe, the sun illuminating whatever is my equivalent of wings. And I now know what I hope my epitaph will be: She wouldn't hurt a fly.

One February, on a freezing sunny day, I walked along the road beside my house. My breath, in clouds, went before me. The winter sun was hard and bright and birch trees wore diamonds.

Donkey kisses have to be taken. They are not given. But they are soft as cotton wool. They come with liquid brown eyes that look at you with mischief. Eyes that, in spite of it all, forgive the wrongs done to them by human ignorance. So gently, and with great care, take a donkey kiss. And consider it a benediction.

'Don't go yet,' I said. 'It's going to rain.'

'How do you know?' the computer whizz asked.

'I looked at the sky,' I answered.

Three minutes later, the sky opened. There are things a laptop just can't tell you.

This morning, a friend and I hung over a half-door, watching a mother hen feeding her chickens. The hen bustled around breaking up bread into crumbs small enough for her tiny, hungry offspring. The clucking sound she made was the essential sound of motherhood, the goodness of the universe was in that little shed.

Before you bash a spider, just stop and think that maybe he is looking at you, saying, 'There's a big awful pink thing with only two legs!' It's all a matter of perspective. Don't destroy what you don't understand.

It is a too-early morning and I cannot sleep.
The day ahead seems too long, too arduous. In my
cold kitchen, I feel like I'm hanging off the edge of
the universe. I challenge myself to wait. To be, in this
uncomfortable uncertainty. Soon the sun will rise.

Curmudgeon

Introduction

There are three things in creation that have no beauty
what-so-ever. None. Nada, zilch. They are things
from hell. They are creations of demons, sent to
drive mankind into foaming-at-the-mouth insanity.
I feel it my duty as an all-seeing, special, guru-type
person to alert you to the satanic properties of:
tights, plastic CD cases and vacuum cleaners.

On the hottest hob in hell, there sits a bitter, twisted female devil. Her sole purpose is to think up ways to torment human females with stupid feckin' tights. She is proud of her work and delights in it since, living in hell, she is allowed a deadly sin or two.

Firstly, she came up with the 'hanging gusset of Babylon'. This instrument of torture not only refuses to go where it should, it scratches the bejaysus out of the thighs of the larger lady. Not content with that, Mrs Demon has instilled in women the irresistible urge to try and correct the gusset-hang with unconscious tight-hoisting.

But this urge doesn't come over you in the privacy of your own home, oh no. Only when you are in a shop — and more likely a posh shop — or the street or, heaven help us, a religious service, do you feel impelled to grab the tight through your outer clothing and yank upwards. It is only when you have completed the yank that you realise what you have done. Mrs Demon has refined the torment even more by supplying a snotty cow who will notice the tight-grappling incident and smirk smugly in your direction. So, red-faced and resisting the urge to rip off the tights and strangle said snotty cow, you go on your way, humiliated.

Next in the demon lady's oeuvre is the 'tantalus tight twist'.

It is a cold winter's morning and you're late for work. You have to get dressed at twice the speed of sound, which you manage to do quite well. Then comes the putting on of the tights. You're on a roll though, so you sit on the edge of the bed, one foot into tights then the other and up they go, hurrah! But no.

Expletives now explode from your mouth, for you have fallen victim to the terrifying tight twist. In your hurry to clothe yourself, you didn't notice that one of the tight legs had been manipulated by Mrs Demon to twist on the way up and now the infernal things cling to your upper thighs like a very determined boa constrictor. You now have a choice. You can go to work and bear the pain and irritation of the tight twist. I advise against this, however, as I have known women who have been arrested for tight rage when doing so. My advice is to sit down and start the process from the beginning. However, then you risk becoming victim to the demon woman's most dastardly invention ... ladies, I present to you Betty Beelzebub's last-minute, finger-poke, reverse ladder.

You have managed to untwist the tight legs and, elated, you hurriedly pull the tights to their last resting place; they're almost there when – zip! Your finger goes through the nylon and ladders travel from your thigh to your ankle with the deadly speed of tidal waves.

By now you are a gibbering wreck. Not helped by the fact that you can faintly hear the cackles of the demon bitch from hell.

This is the Truth of the Tight. Hear it. Believe it. And resolve to wear trousers.

What nitwit thought hard, plastic CD covers were a good idea? If you are able to open one without the CD leaping out and landing wrong side down on the floor, then the thing won't close properly. It's as if all its little quarks have rearranged themselves to be a torture to the poor eejit who just wants to listen to a song. When this happens to me, I tend to go down the route of brute force. Swearing all the swears in my burgeoning lexicon of filthy language, I slam the little fecker shut. Of course, then mass splintering occurs, leaving me with a dangerously exposed CD cowering in its little bed, the top of the case having flown across the room in about twenty pieces.

It doesn't help that most of the CDs I buy are about stress relief. Usually, the upshot of my CD war is finding a copy of 'Embrace Chaos and Live a Peaceful Life' by Someone Rich, languishing in a drawer or a shelf or in the glove compartment of my car, naked and covered in dust and biscuit crumbs. I know I can now acquire music and wisdom without ever going near a CD, but who is going to give me back the bits of my life spent in impotent rage? Now there's a thought for my next book. Reclaiming rage. I can see it all now. Wealth, riches, Oprah Winfrey. Maybe CD covers are a blessing in disguise? No, they are the product of a vile imagination, replete with sadistic machinations dedicated to the destruction of mankind. Well, for me anyway.

Vacuum cleaners. They do my head in. I call the
one I have Purgatory. If there is such a place, I have
lessened my time there by using it. But I think it
probably belongs in Hades. Admittedly it is a cheap
model, but the thoroughbreds of vacuum cleaners are
just as bad. They are all vipers, cocaine-addled vipers.
In the course of my life on earth these serpents of
Satan have wreaked havoc in my house. They have
attacked me on the stairs, rolling down from top to
bottom, only stopping when they have taken the skin
from my shin. When they draw blood they are sated.
They settle on the floor at the bottom of the stairs all
cuddly and innocent, all the time plotting their next
assault. They have destroyed my favourite ornaments.
Let me warn you of this fiendish trick. When you're
not looking, they coil themselves around the flex of
a favourite lamp, something that has nothing to do
with them. When you are in a hurry to have the
house clean for a visitor, you pull on Satan's serpent
to get into a dusty corner, and down comes the
light of your life and it shatters in a million pieces.
You now have to run around sweeping up glass,
worrying that your visitor will bleed to death just

because you invited them for tea. When you have finished your purgatorial penance, you try to put the bloody thing away. You dismantle it into its many cursed parts and try to place it in a corner. Will it stay? Will it heck. You coil the snakey bit, it immediately uncoils. You stack the straight bits against the wall, they fall down. You repeat this process again and again until you are frothing at the mouth like a rabid dog. Eventually, because your visitor has just arrived at the door, you kick it into submission and throw a coat over it, but as you smile in greeting to your guest, you can hear the malevolent hiss and twitch of your nemesis and you know the battle with hell is not over.

Acknowledgements

This little book has been a pleasure to write. More than anything I have done in my creative life, it expresses my true self, not the actress, the performer or the public persona. This is the inside of my head. I try to find meaning in everything: the good, the bad, the seemingly trivial. I have found great meaning in this process and I have people to thank for their midwifery.

Gratitude to Breda Purdue and Hachette for taking another chance on me.

Gratitude to Ciara Doorley for her hands-off but careful stewardship; Ciara, your sense of calm and your sensitive honesty is what made writing this book such a pleasurable experience.

Gratitude to Garvan for the listening, the patience and punctuation!

To Alice Barry for all the *Thelma and Louise* experiences on the road with 'Fruitcake'.

And to Sue, Karen, Helen and the rest of the Lough Crew crew for that magical evening at Samhain.

And gratitude to three women, who, in their listening to me when I was lost, reminded me that the inner life is really the only one that matters. Isobel Mahon, Hazel Revington-Crosse and Martina Stanley.

And finally gratitude, just gratitude.